New Seasons is a trademark of Publications International, Ltd.

© 2005 New Seasons
All rights reserved.
This publication may not be reproduced in whole or in part by any means
whatsoever without written permission from:

Louis Weber, CEO
Publications International, Ltd.
7373 North Cicero Avenue
Lincolnwood, Illinois 60712

www.pilbooks.com

Permission is never granted for commercial purposes.

Manufactured in China.

8 7 6 5 4 3 2 1

ISBN: 1-4127-4779-1

When I'm Old
The Fun Begins

Contributing Writers:
Emily Thornton Calvo
Erika Cornstuble
Alison Pohn
Paul Seaburn

new seasons™

Red hat in the morning,
sailors take warning.

Take a right at the donut shop, then go three blocks, and you'll see a hot dog stand. Take a right there, and go two blocks. Turn left at the pancake place, and you'll see the gym on the corner.

9

My fastball was clocked in the mid-80s. No, wait...that was me!

Mary-Kate and Ashley, consider this a warning.

13

These are nothing. I carried a 200-pound dumbbell for 30 years...then I left him.

Of course I have my good glasses on, honey. Why do you ask?

Who needs a helmet when you know how to use hair spray?

Before we went on our diet,
these were our belts!

The ladies really go
for my butterflies.

By her 13th grandchild,
Ida had become pretty laid-back.

This whole home-shopping thing had gone too far. Janine would either have to give up her stuff or turn in her credit cards.

27

Get me to that yard sale—pronto!

28

29

Forget the tour bus—let's stay here
and watch those hunks clean the pool.

31

Hey! Check out Shirley's
new hip replacement!

Careful, Marshall, or you'll
end up with both sets of teeth.

35

When you said "Watch out for the hot flame," you were referring to me, weren't you?

I got prescription drug coverage!
I got prescription drug coverage!

Do we *look* like desperate housewives?

You do the hokeypokey, and you turn yourself around...

44

Who needs martial arts?
I know Tai Kwan Dough!

45

She just called me a cheater!

47

Oh, no, dear. We don't want to buy insurance. We just wanted some company.

We always suspected Phyllis and Fifi go to the same hairdresser.

52

The older I get, the better
I am at holding my liquor.

Of course we're hippie. Where do you think the weight goes after menopause?

They're his granddaughters, but the boys at the lodge don't have to know.

You're right—the curlers DO give you better reception.

Don't laugh! I get incredible mileage.

Arthur loves to demonstrate the strength of his new denture cream.

Did that trucker just ask me to do
what I think he asked me to do?

He followed me home. Can I keep him?

I taught Eric Clapton all his licks.

I know I used to push you higher, but you used to have less wind resistance.

That wax job I did on your upper arm looks great. Now let's work on your back.

73

Run on the pitch—slide if you have to.

Remember when all we had was a couch and each other? I have a feeling those days are back.